TREASON 2125
OR
WHEN DOES POLITICS
BECOME TREASON

Michael J Carlson

ISBN

Hardcover: 978-1-969120-07-7

Paperback: 978-1-969120-06-0

To:

Citizen and owner of The United States of America

Contents

About the Author

I remember having a very difficult youth. Many problems with mom and dad were common. My personal problems continued in high school until I was kicked out of one high school and dropped out of another.

At 17 years old, my mother and I were locked out of our apartment because we could not pay the rent. We were homeless for a few days until we moved in with my grandmother. As soon as I turned 18, I joined the army.

This was 1969, and the Vietnam War was in progress. My brother was already drafted and in Vietnam when I enlisted. My mother had a problem with me joining the army with my brother already in Vietnam and because of this situation, she had a nervous breakdown.

My personal life began to change once I was in the army. I was trained to be an engineer equipment repairman. Later, I graduated from parachute school and qualified as a paratrooper with 12 parachute jumps, then I attended parachute rigging school to learn how to maintain parachutes. This was the first time in my life I ever graduated from anything. I felt proud of myself.

I remember the American flag back then, serving as a soldier in the United States Army. It took me a while to put all that stuff together because, after all, I was just trying to survive. At 18 years old, to me, it was just a flag and not that much of a big deal. I had to salute it. I had to stand in military formation at attention when the flag was being honored, but I could handle it. This was not that much of a big deal for me until I went to Vietnam. Then, it became a big deal. In fact, the American flag became such a big deal that it remains a big deal to me today. The United States of American stars and stripes are a big fucking deal to me today. Let me explain.

Graduating from parachute school and becoming a paratrooper qualified me to be an engineer equipment repairman for the 173rd Airborne Brigade in Vietnam. I worked in the maintenance shop all day and did perimeter guard duty on the wire 3 to 4 times a week, all night long, guarding helicopters from the bad guys who wanted to come through the wire, cut my throat, and blow up the helicopters. They wanted to do this because I was an American paratrooper for the 173rd Airborne Brigade and they hated American helicopters.

I did this until the 173rd pulled out and went back to the United States. I was transferred to the 101st Airborne Division as a parachute rigger in the northern part of South Vietnam.

As a parachute rigger for the 101st Airborne, one of the things I did was to fly out to a 101st artillery fire base to assist in rigging artillery ammunition.

It was either Artillery Fire Base Bastone or Artillery Fire Base Rifle when this patriotic American stuff really smacked me in the head, and I never forgot it to this day. I was in the middle of the jungle in Vietnam at a 101st Airborne Division artillery base right in the middle of the badlands. And in the middle of the camp was a flag pole with the stars and stripes—the American flag. It was at that time that I never felt prouder to be an American paratrooper from the 101st Airborne Division in Vietnam. To this day, that pride has never left me. I was 20 years old at that time, and today I am 74 years old; I still feel a sense of pride to this day.

I returned from Vietnam and settled in Pasadena, California. This qualified me to attend Pasadena City College, even as a high school dropout. It took me four years to graduate from a two-year junior college and qualified me to attend California State Polytechnic University and study computer information systems.

Graduating from CalPoly, the army hired me as a civilian intern, where I attended and graduated from the U.S. Army Logistics Management College.

Considering my experience at the time, I was a Vietnam veteran of the 173rd Airborne Brigade for nine months and 101st Airborne Division for three months, a graduate from Pasadena City College with a business degree, a graduate of California State Polytechnic University with a computer information systems degree, and a graduate from the U.S. Army Logistics Management College. I felt I could do a lot for the army—and I did.

I helped develop and maintain computer software to forecast helicopter spare parts for Apache and Blackhawk helicopter projects. I was a Systems Programmer working for the Defense Information Systems Agency (DOD), supporting the United States Marines. Later, I developed and maintained office automation and foreign military sales business management software for the same Apache and Blackhawk helicopter projects. As an intern, I was a member of the source selection evaluation board for the Comanche helicopter. Later, I was involved in anti-narcotic business system management for projects in Columbia and an $800 million helicopter program for Kuwait.

For my contributions and service, I was awarded the Army Commendation Medal (ARCOM).

I was able to be this successful because the American system gave me a chance. At 18 years old, I had nothing. The American system allowed me to go from nothing to being successful today. I am a very intense flag-waving American patriot.

I just happen to be the kind of American patriot where American treason really pisses me off.

In America, if you are willing to bust your ass and try, and if in trouble, ask for help and try again and continue to bust your ass in this country, the United States of America, you can be very successful.

Remember the purpose of a problem is to solve the problem.

So, what do you do with treason in America? Solve the problem.

Petition the U.S. Department of Justice for a grand jury investigation into criminal treason and save America.

Michael J. Carlson

Introduction

Greetings, Citizen, and owner of the United States of America.

I believe it is time for us to make our voices heard. I offer and ask for your participation with this online petition addressed to The United States Department of Justice Attorney General to express our concerns for a federal grand jury to investigate reasonable cause for a criminal indictment against whether President Biden, his administration, and others in the Democratic party committed treason against we the people of The United States of America. If The Department of Justice finds reason to believe a probable cause for treason indictments, its procedure should be to ask a federal court to issue arrest warrants, conduct a fair trial, and, if found guilty, deliver an appropriate sentence. Failure to act will leave the opportunity for treason to return and next time we may lose our country.

Failure to arrest the bank robber will result in the bank robber continuing to rob banks.

Remember what Benjamin Franklin said:
"We have a republic if we can keep it."

The Founding Fathers created the Republic; now it is our job to keep it.

Therefore, your participation is required to save The United States of America.

Petition

Current Date: _____

To: To United States Department of Justice
Attorney General
950 Pennsylvania Avenue, NW
Washington, DC 20530-0001

Subject: Request Treason Grand Jury Criminal
Investigation

Purpose:
Whether President Biden, his administration, and
others in the Democratic party committed treason
against us, we the people of the United States of
America from January 2021 through January 2025,
and therefore we ask for a federal grand jury to
investigate reasonable cause for a criminal
indictment and issue, if necessary, against those
responsible.

Failure to act will leave the opportunity for treason
to return and next time we may lose the country.
We asked for your help to save The United States
of America.

Your signature

_____

Your City and State

_____

* * * *   Petition End   * * * *

3

So, please
Use your current date
Sign the document and
include your city and state
Mail To:

U.S. Department of Justice
950 Pennsylvania Avenue, NW
Washington, DC 20530-0001

* * * *   Internet Petition End   * * * *

The purpose of this is to create public interest that will require a Federal Grand Jury to be ordered as required by:

Rule 6. The Grand Jury,
Summoning a Grand Jury,
The Committee on the House of Representatives
December 1, 2024

https://www.uscourts.gov/sites/default/files/2025-02/federal-rules-of-criminal-procedure-dec-1-2024_0.pdf

Shorter Cornell Law School version
https://www.law.cornell.edu/rules/frcrmp/rule_6

FEDERAL RULES
OF
CRIMINAL PROCEDURE
DECEMBER 1, 2024

TITLE III. THE GRAND JURY, THE
INDICTMENT, AND THE
INFORMATION
Rule 6. The Grand Jury
(a) Summoning a Grand Jury.
(1) In General. When the public interest so requires, the
court must order that one or more grand juries be summoned.
A grand jury must have 16 to 23 members, and the court must
order that enough legally qualified persons be summoned to
meet this requirement.

My fellow American, I ask you to sign the petition
and save the United States of America.

The Issue

Statement of issues to be investigated:
The events of the last four years have provided Americans a reason to believe:

1. Treason is in progress.
President Joe Biden, senior members of the executive staff and senior leaders of the Democratic Party, at a minimum, have crossed the line of American Democratic politics only to enter the politics of treason.

2. Under the leadership of President Joe Biden and the American Democratic Party, as well as the senior management of the executive branch of government, the articles of the United States Constitution have been violated.

3. With complete disregard of federal law and order, several federal laws have been violated, resulting in tremendous hardship for the citizens of the United States of America.

4. Under the incompetent and illegal leadership of Homeland Security, supervised and encouraged by President Joe Biden, the historic invasion of the southern border of the United States has been in progress and out of control for the last four years.

5. Due to the refusal of President Biden, the executive branch, the Democratic Party and Homeland Security to provide the necessary resources to defend the United States of America from invasion, the obvious result is treason against the people of the United States for the sole purpose of overthrowing the country, and replacing it with tyranny.

Glossary of Terms

Glossary - Area of Law

Adhering: To hold fast or stick by, to give support or maintain, to bind oneself to observance.

Alien: A person who is not a citizen or national of the United States.

Aid: To provide with what is useful or necessary in achieving an end.

Army: A body of persons organized to advance as a unit to achieve a common goal and objective by force if necessary.

Border: An agreed-upon or legal edge or boundary between two states or countries or cultures or people.

Comfort: To give strength and hope, the knowledge that the program will be fully funded; to ease the grief or trouble.

Democratic: Characterized by or advocating democracy.

Democracy: Government by the people, exercised either directly or through elected representatives.

Enemy: Showing or feeling active hostility, seeking to injure or overthrow by force, if necessary, to achieve their purpose and goals.

Encroach: To enter by gradual steps or by stealth into the possessions or rights of another to advance beyond the usual or proper limits.

Force: Strength or energy exerted or brought to bear: cause of motion or change: active power.

Infringe: To encroach upon in a way that violates law or the rights of another.

Invasion: To enter for conquest or plunder, to encroach upon, to spread over or to permeate through by use of physical force.

Nationality: Loyalty and devotion to a nation; national status; national character

Physical: Characterized or produced by forces and operations.

Principle: Fundamental truth, governing law of conduct, underlying or basic quality that motivates behavior.

Republican: Favoring a republic as the best form of government.

Republic: A government in which the power belongs to a body of citizens entitled to vote, and is exercised by the leaders and representatives elected by those citizens to govern according to law.

Tyranny: Oppressive power exerted by a government in which absolute power is vested in a single ruler or office, authority, and administration of a tyrant

War: A struggle or competition between opposing forces or for a particular end.

The Area of Law

Reference:
https://constitution.congress.gov/constitution/article-3/
United States Constitution

Article III

Section 3

Treason against the United States, shall consist only in levying War against them, or in adhering to their Enemies, giving them Aid and Comfort. No Person shall be convicted of Treason unless on the Testimony of two Witnesses to the same overt Act, or on Confession in open Court.

The Congress shall have Power to declare the Punishment of Treason, but no Attainder of Treason shall work Corruption of Blood, or Forfeiture except during the Life of the Person attainted.

Reference:
https://constitution.congress.gov/constitution/article-4/
United States Constitution

Article IV

Section 4

The United States shall guarantee to every State in this Union a Republican Form of Government, and shall protect each of them against Invasion; and on Application of the Legislature, or of the Executive (when the Legislature cannot be convened) against domestic Violence.

Reference:
https://www.law.cornell.edu/uscode/text/18/2381

18 U.S. Code § 2381 – Treason

Whoever, owing allegiance to the United States, levies war against them or adheres to their enemies, giving them aid and comfort within the United States or elsewhere, is guilty of treason and shall suffer death, or shall be imprisoned not less than five years and fined under this title but not less than $10,000; and shall be incapable of holding any office under the United States.

Reference:
https://www.law.cornell.edu/uscode/text/18/2382

8 U.S. Code §2382. Misprision of treason

Whoever, owing allegiance to the United States and having knowledge of the commission of any treason against them, conceals and does not, as soon as may be, disclose and make known the same to the President or to some judge of the United States, or to the governor or to some judge or justice of a particular State, is guilty of misprision of treason and shall be fined under this title or imprisoned not more than seven years, or both.

Reference:
https://www.law.cornell.edu/uscode/text/8/1325

8 U.S. Code § 1325 Improper entry by alien

(a) Improper time or place; avoidance of examination or inspection; misrepresentation and concealment of facts

13

Any alien who

(1) enters or attempts to enter the United States at any time or place other than as designated by immigration officers, or

(2) eludes examination or inspection by immigration officers, or

(3) attempts to enter or obtains entry to the United States by a willfully false or misleading representation or the willful concealment of a material fact, shall, for the first commission of any such offense, be fined under title 18 or imprisoned not more than 6 months, or both, and, for a subsequent commission of any such offense, be fined under title 18, or imprisoned not more than 2 years, or both.

Reference:
https://www.law.cornell.edu/uscode/text/8/1481
8 U.S. Code § 1481 –

Loss of nationality by native-born or naturalized citizen;

voluntary action; burden of proof; presumptions

(a)A person who is a national of the United States whether by birth or

naturalization, shall lose his nationality by voluntarily performing any of the

following acts with the intention of relinquishing United States nationality—

(7) committing any act of treason against, or attempting by force to overthrow,

or bearing arms against, the United States, violating or conspiring to violate any

of the provisions of section 2383 of title 18, or willfully performing any act in

violation of section 2385 of title 18, or violating section 2384 of title 18 by

engaging in a conspiracy to overthrow, put down, or to destroy by force the

Government of the United States, or to levy war against them, if and when he is

convicted thereof by a court martial or by a court of competent jurisdiction.

The Principle of Law

The fundamental principle of federal law is the Declaration of Independence and the Constitution of the United States.

This is the prime motivation for the creation of the United States of America.

1. Declaration of Independence
Reference: The National Archives.   First two paragraphs:
https://www.archives.gov/founding-docs/declaration-transcript

In Congress, July 4, 1776
The unanimous Declaration of the thirteen United States of America,

When in the Course of human events, it becomes necessary for one people to dissolve the political bands which have connected them with another, and to assume among the powers of the earth, the separate and equal station to which the Laws of Nature and of Nature's God entitle them, a decent respect to the opinions of mankind requires that they should declare the causes which impel them to the separation.

We hold these truths to be self-evident, that all men are created equal, that they are endowed by their

Creator with certain unalienable Rights, that among these are Life, Liberty and the pursuit of Happiness. That to secure these rights, Governments are instituted among Men, deriving their just powers from the consent of the governed, --That whenever any Form of Government becomes destructive of these ends, it is the Right of the People to alter or to abolish it, and to institute new Government, laying its foundation on such principles and organizing its powers in such form, as to them shall seem most likely to effect their Safety and Happiness. Prudence, indeed, will dictate that Governments long established should not be changed for light and transient causes; and accordingly all experience hath shewn, that mankind are more disposed to suffer, while evils are sufferable, than to right themselves by abolishing the forms to which they are accustomed. But when a long train of abuses and usurpations, pursuing invariably the same Object evinces a design to reduce them under absolute Despotism, it is their right, it is their duty, to throw off such Government, and to provide new Guards for their future security.--Such has been the patient sufferance of these Colonies; and such is now the necessity which constrains them to alter their former Systems of Government. The history of the present King of Great Britain is a history of repeated injuries and usurpations, all having in direct object the establishment of an absolute Tyranny over these States. To prove this, let Facts be submitted to a candid world.

2. Constitution of the United States
Ratification of the Conventions of Nine States
September 17,1787
Reference: The National Archives.
https://www.archives.gov/founding-docs/constitution-transcript

The Articles are the primary legal leadership and guidance to American Law
Preamble Introduction

We the People of the United States, in Order to form a more perfect Union, establish Justice, insure domestic Tranquility, provide for the common defense, promote the general Welfare, and secure the Blessings of Liberty to ourselves and our Posterity, do ordain and establish this Constitution for the United States of America.

Since September 17, 1787, the Articles are and have been the primary leadership and guidance to American Law.

Synopsis of Evidence

List Table of Contents

Evidence Number 1
Reference:
https://www.presidency.ucsb.edu/documents/executi
ve-order-13768-enhancing-public-safety-the-
interior-the-united-states

President Donald J. Trump
Subject: Executive Order 13768—Enhancing Public
Safety in the Interior of the United States
January 25, 2017 Border Policy General description
of 18 sections of executive actions to include:

Section 1. Purpose,

Sec. 2. Policy,

Sec. 3. Definitions,

Sec.4. Enforcement of the Immigration Laws in the Interior of the United States,

Sec. 5. Enforcement Priorities,

Sec. 6. Civil Fines and Penalties,

Sec. 7. Additional Enforcement and Removal Officers.

Sec. 8. Federal-State Agreements,

Sec. 9. Sanctuary Jurisdictions.

Sec. 10. Review of Previous Immigration Actions and Policies.

Sec. 11. Department of Justice Prosecutions of Immigration Violators.

Sec. 12. Recalcitrant Countries.

20

Sec. 13. Office for Victims of Crimes Committed by Removable Aliens.

Sec. 14. Privacy Act

Sec. 15. Reporting

Sec. 16. Transparency

Sec. 17. Personnel Actions, Sec. 18. General Provisions.

Evidence Number 2
Reference:
https://www.presidency.ucsb.edu/documents/executi ve-order-13993-revision-civil-immigration-enforcement-policies-and-priorities

Executive Order 13993—Revision of Civil Immigration Enforcement Policies and Priorities
President Joseph R. Biden
January 20, 2021 Reverse Border Policy

Section 1. Policy. Immigrants

Section 2. Revocation Executive Order 13768 of January 25, 2017

Section 3. General Provisions.

January 20, 2021

Evidence Number 3
Reference:
https://gov.texas.gov/uploads/files/press/BidenJoseph_11.16.22.pdf

From: Governor Greg Abbott of Texas

To: President Joe Biden

Topic: Article IV, § 4, that the federal government "shall protect each of them against Invasion. Texans are paying the price for your failure.
November 16, 2022

Evidence Number 4
Reference:
https://gov.texas.gov/uploads/files/press/O-AgencyHeads202209200176.pdf

From: TEXAS GOVERNOR GREG ABBOTT

To: Texas Commissioners and Directors

Subject: Facing a Fentanyl crisis.
September 20, 2022

Evidence Number 5
Reference:
https://gov.texas.gov/uploads/files/press/President_J
oseph_R._Biden_sig_.pdf

Letter to President Joseph R. Biden, Jr

From: Greg Abbott Governor of Texas

Topic: … violating your constitutional obligation to defend the States against invasion through faithful execution of federal laws

January 8, 2023

Evidence Number 6
Reference:
https://gov.texas.gov/uploads/files/press/County_Ju
dge_Invasion_Letter.pdf

From: Greg Abbott Governor of Texas

To: County Judges
Topic: Defending Texas Against Invasion

November 14, 2022

Evidence Number 7
Reference:
https://gov.texas.gov/uploads/files/press/Colonel_St
even_McCraw_Major_General_Thomas_Suelzer.pd
f
From: Greg Abbott Governor of Texas

To: Major General Thomas M. Suelzer, Colonel
Steven C. McCraw
Topic: the Texas National Guard have been given the
enormous task of securing our Texas border

November 16, 2022

Evidence Number 8
Reference:

https://judiciary.house.gov/sites/evo-
subsites/republicans-
judiciary.house.gov/files/legacy_files/wp-
content/uploads/2022/11/2022-11-18-HJC-GOP-to-
Garland-DOJ.pdf

From: U.S. Congress House of Representatives
Committee on the Judiciary

Topic: Congress Request Refused

To: The Honorable Merrick B. Garland
Attorney General
U.S. Department of Justice
November 18, 2022

Evidence Number 9
Reference:
https://www.rga.org/wp-
content/uploads/2021/09/Joint-Letter-to-President-
Biden-to-meet-on-Border-09.20.21.pdf

To: President Joseph R. Biden, Jr.
From 26 State Governors

Topic: ... crisis that began at our southern border now extends beyond to every state and requires immediate action before the situation worsens.

September 20, 2021

Evidence Number 10
Reference:
https://www.federalregister.gov/documents/2025/01/29/2025-01948/declaring-a-national-emergency-at-the-southern-border-of-the-united-states

From: Donald Trump
Proclamation 10886 of January 20, 2025
Declaring a National Emergency at the Southern Border of the United States

The Evidence

Number 1

1. Reference:
https://www.presidency.ucsb.edu/documents/executive-order-13768-enhancing-public-safety-the-interior-the-united-states

Executive Order 13768—Enhancing Public Safety in the Interior of the United States
President Donald J. Trump
January 25, 2017 Border Policy

Executive Order 13768 of January 25, 2017

Enhancing Public Safety in the Interior of the United States

By the authority vested in me as President by the Constitution and the laws of the United States of America, including the Immigration and Nationality Act (INA) (8 U.S.C. 1101 et seq.), and in order to ensure the public safety of the American people in communities across the United States as well as to ensure that our Nation's immigration laws are faithfully executed, I hereby declare the policy of the executive branch to be, and order, as follows:

Section 1 . Purpose. Interior enforcement of our Nation's immigration laws is critically important to the national security and public safety of the United States. Many aliens who illegally enter the United States and those who overstay or otherwise violate the terms of their visas present a significant threat to national security and public safety. This is particularly so for aliens who engage in criminal conduct in the United States.

Sanctuary jurisdictions across the United States willfully violate Federal law in an attempt to shield aliens from removal from the United States. These jurisdictions have caused immeasurable harm to the American people and to the very fabric of our Republic.

Tens of thousands of removable aliens have been released into communities across the country, solely because their home countries refuse to accept their repatriation. Many of these aliens are criminals who have served time in our Federal, State, and local jails. The presence of such individuals in the United States, and the practices of foreign nations that refuse the repatriation of their nationals, are contrary to the national interest.

Although Federal immigration law provides a framework for Federal-State partnerships in enforcing our immigration laws to ensure the removal of aliens who have no right to be in the United States, the Federal Government has failed to discharge this basic sovereign responsibility. We cannot faithfully execute the immigration laws of the United States if we exempt classes or categories of removable aliens from potential enforcement. The purpose of this order is to direct executive departments and agencies (agencies) to employ all lawful means to enforce the immigration laws of the United States.

Sec. 2, Policy. It is the policy of the executive branch to:

(a) Ensure the faithful execution of the immigration laws of the United States, including the INA, against all removable aliens, consistent with Article II, Section 3 of the United States Constitution, and section 3331 of title 5, United States Code;

(b) Make use of all available systems and resources to ensure the efficient and faithful execution of the immigration laws of the United States;

(c) Ensure that jurisdictions that fail to comply with applicable Federal law do not receive Federal funds, except as mandated by law;

(d) Ensure that aliens ordered removed from the United States are promptly removed; and

(e) Support victims, and the families of victims, of crimes committed by removable aliens.

Sec. 3 . Definitions. The terms of this order, where applicable, shall have the meaning provided by section 1101 of title 8, United States Code.

Sec. 4 . Enforcement of the Immigration Laws in the Interior of the United States.

In furtherance of the policy described in section 2 of this order, I hereby direct agencies to employ all lawful means to ensure the faithful execution of the immigration laws of the United States against all removable aliens.

Sec. 5 Enforcement Priorities. In executing faithfully the immigration laws of the United States, the Secretary of Homeland Security (Secretary) shall prioritize for removal those aliens described by the Congress in sections 212(a)(2), (a)(3), and (a)(6)(C), 235, and 237(a)(2) and (4) of the INA (8 U.S.C. 1182(a)(2), (a)(3), and (a)(6)(C), 1225, and 1227(a)(2) and (4)), as well as removable aliens who:

(a) Have been convicted of any criminal offense;

(b) Have been charged with any criminal offense, where such charge has not been resolved;

(c) Have committed acts that constitute a chargeable criminal offense;

(d) Have engaged in fraud or willful misrepresentation in connection with any official matter or application before a governmental agency;

(e) Have abused any program related to receipt of public benefits;

(f) Are subject to a final order of removal, but who have not complied with their legal obligation to depart the United States; or

(g) In the judgment of an immigration officer, otherwise pose a risk to public safety or national security.

Sec. 6 Civil Fines and Penalties. As soon as practicable, and by no later than one year after the date of this order, the Secretary shall issue guidance and promulgate regulations, where required by law, to ensure the assessment and collection of all fines and penalties that the Secretary is authorized under the law to assess and collect from aliens unlawfully present in the United States and from those who facilitate their presence in the United States.

Sec. 7 Additional Enforcement and Removal Officers. The Secretary, through the Director of U.S. Immigration and Customs Enforcement, shall, to the extent permitted by law and subject to the availability of appropriations, take all appropriate action to hire 10,000 additional immigration officers, who shall complete relevant training and be authorized to perform the law enforcement functions described in section 287 of the INA (8 U.S.C. 1357).

Sec. 8 Federal-State Agreements. It is the policy of the executive branch to empower State and local law enforcement agencies across the country to perform the functions of an immigration officer in the interior of the United States to the maximum extent permitted by law.

(a) In furtherance of this policy, the Secretary shall immediately take appropriate action to engage with the Governors of the States, as well as local officials, for the purpose of preparing to enter into agreements under section 287(g) of the INA (8 U.S.C. 1357(g)).

(b) To the extent permitted by law and with the consent of State or local officials, as appropriate, the Secretary shall take appropriate action, through agreements under section 287(g) of the INA, or otherwise, to authorize State and local law enforcement officials, as the Secretary determines are qualified and appropriate, to perform the functions of immigration officers in relation to the investigation, apprehension, or detention of aliens in the United States under the direction and the supervision of the Secretary. Such authorization shall be in addition to, rather than in place of, Federal performance of these duties.

(c) To the extent permitted by law, the Secretary may structure each agreement under section 287(g) of the INA in a manner that provides the most effective model for enforcing Federal immigration laws for that jurisdiction.

Sec. 9 Sanctuary Jurisdictions.

It is the policy of the executive branch to ensure, to the fullest extent of the law, that a State, or a political subdivision of a State, shall comply with 8 U.S.C. 1373.

(a) In furtherance of this policy, the Attorney General and the Secretary, in their discretion and to the extent consistent with law, shall ensure that jurisdictions that willfully refuse to comply with 8 U.S.C. 1373 (sanctuary jurisdictions) are not eligible to receive Federal grants, except as deemed necessary for law enforcement purposes by the Attorney General or the Secretary. The Secretary has the authority to designate, in his discretion and to the extent consistent with law, a jurisdiction as a sanctuary jurisdiction. The Attorney General shall take appropriate enforcement action against any entity that violates 8 U.S.C. 1373, or which has in effect a statute, policy, or practice that prevents or hinders the enforcement of Federal law.

(b) To better inform the public regarding the public safety threats associated with sanctuary jurisdictions, the Secretary shall utilize the Declined Detainer

Outcome Report or its equivalent and, on a weekly basis, make public a comprehensive list of criminal actions committed by aliens and any jurisdiction that ignored or otherwise failed to honor any detainers with respect to such aliens.

(c) The Director of the Office of Management and Budget is directed to obtain and provide relevant and responsive information on all Federal grant money that currently is received by any sanctuary jurisdiction.

Sec. 10 Review of Previous Immigration Actions and Policies

(a) The Secretary shall immediately take all appropriate action to terminate the Priority Enforcement Program (PEP) described in the memorandum issued by the Secretary on November 20, 2014, and to reinstitute the immigration program known as "Secure Communities" referenced in that memorandum.

(b) The Secretary shall review agency regulations, policies, and procedures for consistency with this order and, if required, publish for notice and comment proposed regulations rescinding or revising any regulations inconsistent with this order and shall consider whether to withdraw or modify any inconsistent policies and procedures, as appropriate and consistent with the law.

(c) To protect our communities and better facilitate the identification, detention, and removal of criminal aliens within constitutional and statutory parameters, the Secretary shall consolidate and revise any applicable forms to more effectively communicate with recipient law enforcement agencies.

Sec. 11. Department of Justice Prosecutions of Immigration Violators.

The Attorney General and the Secretary shall work together to develop and implement a program that ensures that adequate resources are devoted to the prosecution of criminal immigration offenses in the United States, and to develop cooperative strategies to reduce violent crime and the reach of transnational criminal organizations into the United States.

Sec. 12. Recalcitrant Countries. The Secretary of Homeland Security and the Secretary of State shall cooperate to effectively implement the sanctions provided by section 243(d) of the INA (8 U.S.C. 1253(d)), as appropriate. The Secretary of State shall, to the maximum extent permitted by law, ensure that diplomatic efforts and negotiations with foreign states include as a condition precedent the acceptance by those foreign states of their nationals who are subject to removal from the United States.

Sec. 13. Office for Victims of Crimes Committed by Removable Aliens. The Secretary shall direct the Director of U.S. Immigration and Customs

Enforcement to take all appropriate and lawful action to establish within U.S. Immigration and Customs Enforcement an office to provide proactive, timely, adequate, and professional services to victims of crimes committed by removable aliens and the family members of such victims. This office shall provide quarterly reports studying the effects of the victimization by criminal aliens present in the United States.

Sec. 14. Privacy Act. Agencies shall, to the extent consistent with applicable law, ensure that their privacy policies exclude persons who are not United States citizens or lawful permanent residents from the protections of the Privacy Act regarding personally identifiable information.

Sec. 15. Reporting. Except as otherwise provided in this order, the Secretary and the Attorney General shall each submit to the President a report on the progress of the directives contained in this order within 90 days of the date of this order and again within 180 days of the date of this order.

Sec. 16. Transparency. To promote the transparency and situational awareness of criminal aliens in the United States, the Secretary and the Attorney General are hereby directed to collect relevant data and provide quarterly reports on the following:

(a) the immigration status of all aliens incarcerated under the supervision of the Federal Bureau of Prisons;

(b) the immigration status of all aliens incarcerated as Federal pretrial detainees under the supervision of the United States Marshals Service; and

(c) the immigration status of all convicted aliens incarcerated in State prisons and local detention centers throughout the United States.

Sec. 17. Personnel Actions. The Office of Personnel Management shall take appropriate and lawful action to facilitate hiring personnel to implement this order.

Sec. 18. General Provisions. (a) Nothing in this order shall be construed to impair or otherwise affect:

(i)the authority granted by law to an executive department or agency, or the head thereof; or

(ii)the functions of the Director of the Office of Management and Budget relating to budgetary, administrative, or legislative proposals.

(b)This order shall be implemented consistent with applicable law and subject to the availability of appropriations.

(c) This order is not intended to, and does not, create any right or benefit, substantive or procedural, enforceable at law or in equity by any party against the United States, its departments, agencies, or entities, its officers, employees, or agents, or any other person.

DONALD J. TRUMP

THE WHITE HOUSE,

January 25, 2017.

NOTE: This Executive order was published in the Federal Register on January 30.

------- The Evidence Number 1 ------

The Evidence

2. Reference:
https://www.presidency.ucsb.edu/documents/executive-order-13993-revision-civil-immigration-enforcement-policies-and-priorities

Executive Order 13993—Revision of Civil Immigration Enforcement Policies and Priorities President Joseph R. Biden

January 20, 2021 Reverse Border Policy January 25, 2017

Joseph R. Biden, Jr.
46th President of the United States: 2021—2025
Executive Order 13993—Revision of Civil Immigration Enforcement Policies and Priorities

By the authority vested in me as President by the Constitution and the laws of the United States of America, it is hereby ordered as follows:

Section 1. Policy. Immigrants have helped strengthen America's families, communities, businesses and workforce, and economy, infusing the United States with creativity, energy, and ingenuity. The task of enforcing the immigration laws is complex and requires setting priorities to best serve the national interest. The policy of my Administration is to protect national and border security, address the humanitarian challenges at the southern border, and ensure public health and safety. We must also adhere to due process of law as we safeguard the dignity and well-being of all families and communities. My Administration will reset the policies and practices for enforcing civil immigration laws to align enforcement with these values and priorities.

Sec. 2. Revocation. Executive Order 13768 of January 25, 2017 (Enhancing Public Safety in the Interior of the United States), is hereby revoked. The Secretary of State, the Attorney General, the Secretary of Homeland Security, the Director of the Office of Management and Budget, the Director of the Office of Personnel Management, and the heads of any other relevant executive departments and agencies (agencies) shall review any agency actions developed pursuant to Executive Order 13768 and take action, including issuing revised guidance, as appropriate and consistent with applicable law, that advances the policy set forth in section 1 of this order.

Sec. 3. General Provisions.

 (a) Nothing in this order shall be construed to impair or otherwise affect:

(i) the authority granted by law to an executive department or agency, or the head thereof; or

(ii) the functions of the Director of the Office of Management and Budget relating to budgetary, administrative, or legislative proposals.

(b) This order shall be implemented consistent with applicable law and subject to the availability of appropriations.

(c) This order is not intended to, and does not, create any right or benefit, substantive, or procedural, enforceable at law or in equity by any party against the United States, its departments, agencies, or entities, its officers, employees, or agents, or any other person.

Signature of Joe Biden
JOSEPH R. BIDEN, JR.
The White House,
January 20, 2021.

NOTE: This Executive order was published in the Federal Register on January 25.

Joseph R. Biden, Jr., Executive Order 13993—Revision of Civil Immigration Enforcement Policies and Priorities Online by Gerhard Peters and John T. Woolley, The American Presidency Project https://www.presidency.ucsb.edu/node/347817

------- The Evidence Number 2 ------

41

The Evidence

Number 3

3. Reference:
https://gov.texas.gov/uploads/files/press/BidenJoseph_11.16.22.pdf

GOVERNOR GREG ABBOTT
November 16, 2022
The Honorable Joseph R. Biden, Jr.
President of the United States
The White House
1600 Pennsylvania Avenue NW
Washington, D.C. 20500

Dear President Biden:

The U.S. Constitution won ratification by promising the States, in Article IV, § 4, that the federal government "shall protect each of them against Invasion." By refusing to enforce the immigration laws enacted by Congress, including 8 U.S.C. § 1325(a)(1)'s criminal prohibition against aliens entering the United States between authorized ports of entry, your Administration has made clear that it will not honor that guarantee. The federal government's failure has forced me to invoke Article I, § 10, Clause 3 of the U.S. Constitution, thereby enabling the State of Texas to protect its own territory against invasion by the Mexican drug cartels.

Your inaction has led to catastrophic consequences. Under your watch, America is suffering the highest volume of illegal immigration in the history of our country. This past year, more than 2 million immigrants tried to enter the country illegally, coming from more than 100 countries across the globe. Worse yet, your failed border policies recently prompted a United Nations agency to declare that the border between the United States and Mexico is the deadliest land crossing in the world.

Texans are paying the price for your failure. Ranches are being ripped apart, and homes are vulnerable to intrusion. Our border communities are regularly disrupted by human traffickers and bailouts. Deadly fentanyl is crossing the porous border to such a degree that it is now the leading cause of death for citizens between the ages of 18 and 45.

By opening our border to this record-breaking level of illegal immigration, you and your Administration are in violation of Article IV, § 4 of the U.S. Constitution. Your sustained dereliction of duty compels Texas to invoke the powers reserved in Article I, § 10, Clause 3, which represents "an acknowledgement of the States' sovereign interest in protecting their borders." Arizona v. United States, 567 U.S. 387, 419 (2012) (Scalia, J., dissenting). Using that authority, Texas will escalate our efforts to repel and turn back any immigrant who seeks to enter our State at a border crossing that Congress has designated as illegal; to return to the border those who do cross illegally; and to arrest criminals who violate Texas law.

Know this: Article I, § 10, Clause 3 is not just excess verbiage. It reflects an understanding by our Founders, the authors of the Constitution, that some future President might abandon his obligation to safeguard the States from an extraordinary inflow of people who have no legal right of entry. They foresaw your failures. In the more than 240 years of our great nation, no Administration has done more than yours to place the States in "imminent Danger"—a direct result of your policy decisions and refusal to deliver on the Article IV, § 4 guarantee. In the absence of action by your Administration to secure the border, every act by Texas officials is taken pursuant to the authority that the Founders recognized in Article I, § 10, Clause 3.

All of this can be avoided, of course, if you will simply enforce the laws that are already on the books. Your Administration must end its catch-and-release policies, repel this unprecedented mass migration, and satisfy its constitutional obligation through faithful execution of the immigration laws enacted by Congress:

• You should aggressively prosecute the federal crimes of illegal entry and illegal reentry. See 8 U.S.C. § 1325, § 1326.

• You should comply with statutes mandating that various categories of aliens "shall" be detained. See, e.g., 8 U.S.C. § 1225(b)(1)(B)(ii) & (iii)(IV) (aliens claiming asylum); id. § 1225(b)(2)(A) (aliens applying for admission); id. § 1226(c)(1) (criminal aliens); id. § 1231(a)(2) (aliens ordered removed); id. § 1222(a) (aliens who may carry disease).

• You should stop paroling aliens end masse in violation of the Illegal Immigration Reform and Immigrant Responsibility Act of 1996, which decrees that aliens applying for admission can be paroled into the United States "only on a case-by-case basis for urgent humanitarian reasons or significant public benefit." 8 U.S.C. § 1182(d)(5)(A).

• You should fully reinstate the Migrant Protection Protocols, such that aliens seeking admission remain in Mexico while proceedings unfold in the United States. See 8 U.S.C. § 1225(b)(2)(C).

• You should immediately resume construction of the border wall in Texas, using the billions of dollars Congress has appropriated for that purpose. See FY2021 DHS Appropriations Act § 210, Pub. L. 116-260, 134 Stat. 1182, 1456–57 (Dec. 27, 2020); FY2020 DHS Appropriations Act § 209, Pub. L. 116-93, 133 Stat. 2317, 2511–12 (Dec. 20, 2019).

Americans want an orderly immigration process that adheres to the laws enacted by the legislators they sent to Washington. In the words of Judge Oldham, however, you have "supplant[ed] the rule of law with the rule of say-so" while "tell[ing] Congress to pound sand." Texas v. Biden, 20 F.4th 928, 982, 1004 (5th Cir. 2021); cf. U.S. CONST. art. I, § 8, cl. 4 (empowering Congress "[t]o establish an uniform Rule of Naturalization")

Before you took office, the United States enjoyed some of the lowest illegal-immigration figures it had seen in decades. Your Administration gutted the policies that yielded those low numbers. You must reinstate the policies that you eliminated, or craft and implement new policies, in order to fulfill your constitutional duty to enforce federal immigration laws and protect the States against invasion.

Your silence in the face of our repeated pleas is deafening. Your refusal to even visit the border for a firsthand look at the chaos you have caused is damning. Two years of inaction on your part now leave Texas with no choice but to escalate our efforts to secure our State. Your open-border policies, which have catalyzed an unprecedented crisis of illegal immigration, are the sole cause of Texas having to invoke our constitutional authority to defend ourselves.

Sincerely,

Greg Abbott Governor of Texas
GA:jsd

cc: The Honorable Merrick B. Garland, U.S. Attorney General

The Honorable Alejandro Mayorkas, U.S. Secretary of Homeland Security

------- The Evidence Number 3 ------

The Evidence

4. Reference:
https://gov.texas.gov/uploads/files/press/O-AgencyHeads202209200176.pdf
From:
TEXAS GOVERNOR GREG ABBOTT
September 20, 2022

To:
Mr. Mike H. Morath
Commissioner
Texas Education Agency
1701 North Congress Avenue
Austin, Texas 78701

Ms. Cecile Young
Executive Commissioner
Health and Human Services Commission
P.O. Box 13247
Austin, Texas 78711-3247

Ms. Jaime Masters
Commissioner
Department of Family and Protective Services
701 West 51st Street

Austin, Texas 78751

Dr. Harrison Keller
Commissioner
Texas Higher Education Coordinating Board
P.O. Box 12788
Austin, Texas 78711-2788

Mr. Brian Collier
Executive Director
Texas Department of Criminal Justice
P.O. Box 13084
Austin, Texas 78711-3084

Colonel Steven C. McCraw
Director
Department of Public Safety
P.O. Box 4087
Austin, Texas 78773-0001

Dr. John Hellerstedt
Commissioner
Department of State Health Services
P.O. Box 149347
Austin, Texas 78714-9347

Ms. Shandra Carter
Interim Executive Director

Texas Juvenile Justice Department
11209 Metric Boulevard
Austin, Texas 78758

Mr. Ed Serna
Executive Director
Texas Workforce Commission
101 East 15th Street
Austin, Texas 78778-0001

Dear Agency Heads:

As you know, our nation is facing a fentanyl crisis. Fentanyl is a synthetic opioid that is 50–100 times more potent than morphine, often proving lethal with as little as 2 milligrams. Over 71,000 Americans died from fentanyl in 2021, an increase of 23 percent from the previous year. Over that same period, Texas saw an 89 percent increase in fentanyl-related deaths, with provisional data showing 1,672 such tragedies in 2021, compared to 883 of them in 2020. These are steep increases since 2018, when there were 214 fentanyl-related deaths in Texas.

It has become clear that fentanyl is impacting individuals with and without substance use disorders. Unfortunately, most individuals who suffer a fentanyl-related death probably did not know they were ingesting the deadly drug. Many of those who were poisoned unwittingly ingested deadly counterfeits that appeared to be prescription drugs, which were acquired outside of the healthcare system. Most fentanyl in Texas is produced by Mexican drug cartels that combine fentanyl with other drugs. Many of those drugs look like and are marketed by drug traffickers as legitimate prescription painkillers, stimulants, or anti-anxiety drugs. Even more devious is "rainbow fentanyl," which is made to look like candy so it can be marketed to children. Simply put, fentanyl is a clandestine killer, and Texans are falling victim to the cartels that are producing it.

Due to the threats posed by an open border and in the absence of federal action, I initiated Operation Lone Star on March 4, 2021. Since that time, the Texas Department of Public Safety (DPS) has seized more than 336 million lethal doses of fentanyl across the state. That is enough fentanyl to kill every man, woman, and child in the United States. The efforts of DPS are noteworthy and commendable, but law enforcement alone cannot be expected to end this crisis.

Fentanyl's potency and deceptiveness, combined with the federal government's unwillingness to take border security seriously, pose a grave threat to Texans. We must take all appropriate actions to inform Texans of this danger and prevent additional deaths. To this end, I am directing each of your agencies to inform the populations you serve of fentanyl's lethality and prevalence. Actions could include, but are not limited to, developing public service announcements, posting flyers in prominent locations around regulated facilities, training staff, or providing educational opportunities to the people you serve.

Furthermore, the state must also look for ways to enhance all aspects of the state's response to this crisis. As the Texas Legislature prepares to meet in January 2023, agencies should be prepared to outline statutory changes, budget priorities, and other initiatives that will enhance the state's ability to interdict this dangerous drug, provide emergency overdose treatment, and expand substance abuse treatment programs. These agency efforts can be amplified by strategic coordination with the Texas Opioid Abatement Fund Council. I appreciate Comptroller Glen Hegar for inviting many of you to the next council meeting to present your current efforts to protect Texans from controlled substances.

Thank you for the work you and your colleagues do, and thank you for taking this issue seriously. Together we can help bring awareness to the threat posed by fentanyl and do our part to address this crisis.

Sincerely,
Greg Abbott
Governor
GA:shd

cc: Comptroller Glen Hegar

------- End Reference 4 ------

The Evidence

5. Reference:
https://gov.texas.gov/uploads/files/press/President_J
oseph_R._Biden_sig_.pdf

Letter to President Joseph R. Biden, Jr.
From: Greg Abbott Governor of Texas
January 8, 2023

The Honorable Joseph R. Biden, Jr.
President of the United States

Dear President Biden:

Your visit to our southern border with Mexico today
is $20 billion too little and two years too late.
Moreover, your visit avoids the sites where mass
illegal immigration occurs and sidesteps the
thousands of angry Texas property owners whose
lives have been destroyed by your border policies.
Even the city you visit has been sanitized of the
migrant camps which had overrun downtown El Paso
because your Administration wants to shield you
from the chaos that Texans experience on a daily
basis. This chaos is the direct result of your failure
to enforce the immigration laws that Congress
enacted.

Under President Trump, the federal government achieved historically low levels of illegal immigration. Under your watch, by contrast, America is suffering the worst illegal immigration in the history of our country. Your open-border policies have emboldened the cartels, who grow wealthy by trafficking deadly fentanyl and even human beings. Texans are paying an especially high price for your failure, sometimes with their very lives, as local leaders from your own party will tell you if given the chance.

All of this is happening because you have violated your constitutional obligation to defend the States against invasion through faithful execution of federal laws. Halfway through your presidency, though, I can finally welcome you to the border. When you finish the photo-ops in a carefully stage-managed version of El Paso, you have a job to do:

• You must comply with the many statutes mandating that various categories of aliens

"shall" be detained, and end the practice of unlawfully paroling aliens en masse.

• You must stop sandbagging the implementation of the Remain-in-Mexico policy and

Title 42 expulsions, and fully enforce those measures as the federal courts have ordered you to do.

• You must aggressively prosecute illegal entry between ports of entry, and allow ICE to remove illegal immigrants in accordance with existing federal laws.

• You must immediately resume construction of the border wall in the State of Texas, using the billions of dollars Congress has appropriated for that purpose.

• You must designate the Mexican drug cartels as foreign terrorist organizations.

On behalf of all Americans, I implore you: Secure our border by enforcing Congress's immigration laws.

Sincerely,
Greg Abbott
Governor

POSTOFFICE   BOX12428   AUSTIN, TEXAS78711512-463-2000(VOICE)DIAL7-1-1FORRELAYSERVICE

------- End Reference 5 ------

55

The Evidence

6. Reference:
https://gov.texas.gov/uploads/files/press/County_Ju
dge_Invasion_Letter.pdf

GOVERNOR GREG ABBOTT
November 14, 2022

Re: Defending Texas Against Invasion

Dear County Judge;

Thank you for the letter from your county expressing support for what Texas is doing to secure the border. As you know, President Biden has abandoned his responsibility to enforce immigration laws, and Congress has refused to hold the President accountable and has abandoned its own responsibility to use the immigration power given to it in Article I, § 8 of the U.S. Constitution.

Just two years ago, we had the fewest illegal crossings in decades. This past year under President Biden, an all-time record was set for the number of immigrants crossing the border illegally.

Texas has forcefully responded to Biden's open border policies by doing more than any state in the history of America to do the federal government's job to secure the border.

In my Executive Order GA-41, I invoked the Invasion Clauses of Article I, § 10 of the U.S. Constitution and Article IV, § 7 of the Texas Constitution to fully authorize Texas to take unprecedented measures to fight back against the invasion at our border. As Governor of Texas and commander-in-chief of its military forces, I am using that constitutional authority, as well as other authorization and Executive Orders to:

• Deploy the National Guard to safeguard our border and to repel and turn back immigrants trying to cross
the border illegally;

• Deploy the Texas Department of Public Safety (DPS) to arrest and return to the border immigrants who crossed illegally and deploy DPS to arrest illegal immigrants for criminal activity;

• Build a border wall in multiple counties on the border;

• Deploy gun boats to secure the border;

• Designate Mexican drug cartels as foreign terrorist organizations;

• Enter into a compact with other states to secure the border;

- Enter into agreements with foreign powers to enhance border security; and

- Provide resources for border counties to increase their efforts to respond to the border invasion.

POST OFFICE BOX 12428AUSTIN, TEXAS 78711 512-463-2000 (VOICE) DIAL 7-1-1 FOR RELAY SERVICES

County Judges
November 14, 2022
Page 2

Texas has devoted more than $4 billion of Texas taxpayer dollars toward these and other efforts to secure the border and enhance public safety.

In January 2023 when the next Congress is sworn in, we must remind our representatives in Washington that securing the border is the federal government's responsibility under Article I, § 8 and Article IV, § 4 of the U.S. Constitution. Congress should reimburse the State of Texas for the billions of dollars we have had to spend on border security in the Biden Administration's absence. Federal officials who will not faithfully execute the immigrations laws should face hearings and even impeachment. Finally, Congress should amend statutes like 18 U.S.C. § 242 to ensure that our Troopers and Guardsmen are not exposed to federal criminal prosecution for protecting Texas against illegal entry between the ports of entry.

Join me in sending this urgent message to our congressional delegation, which has the power to act under Article I, § 8 of the U.S. Constitution. Texas has done more than its fair share for far too long. The time has come for the federal government to do its job.

Greg Abbott

Governor

GA:mhd

------- End Reference 6 ------

The Evidence

7. Reference:
https://gov.texas.gov/uploads/files/press/Colonel_St
even_McCraw_Major_General_Thomas_Suelzer.pd
f

GOVERNOR GREG ABBOTT
November 16, 2022

Colonel Steven C. McCraw
Director
Department of Public Safety
P.O. Box 4087
Austin, Texas 78773-0001

Major General Thomas M. Suelzer
Adjutant General
Texas Military Department
P.O. Box 5218
Austin, Texas 78703

Re: Defend Texas Against Invasion

Dear Colonel McCraw and General Suelzer:

Since the launch of Operation Lone Star in March 2021, the Texas Department of Public Safety (DPS) and the Texas National Guard have been given the enormous task of securing our Texas border. Over the course of the last year and a half, I authorized Texas Guardsmen and Troopers to repel and turnback immigrants trying to cross the border illegally; arrest and return to the border immigrants who have crossed illegally; and arrest criminal trespassers and those violating Texas law. The number of drug traffickers and human traffickers you have arrested is astonishing. The wave of fentanyl and criminals you have stopped from entering the United States by way of the border is shocking. I thank you for the unprecedented work your

Guardsmen and Troopers have done on Operation Lone Star. This work must continue and now be expanded upon.

As you know, these efforts have been required of Texas because President Biden has abandoned his responsibility to enforce immigration laws, and Congress has refused to hold the President accountable and has abandoned its own responsibility to use the immigration power given to it in Article I, § 8 of the U.S. Constitution.

Attached are copies of a letter I sent to several Texas county leaders detailing the actions we have taken to secure the border. This includes my Executive Order GA-41, in which I invoked the Invasion Clauses of Article I, § 10 of the U.S. Constitution and Article IV,

§ 7 of the Texas Constitution to fully authorize Texas to take unprecedented measures to fight back against the

POST OFFICE BOX 12428AUSTIN, TEXAS 78711 512-463-2000 (VOICE) DIAL 7-1-1 FOR RELAY SERVICES

Colonel Steven C. McCraw
Major General Thomas M. Suelzer
November 16, 2022

Page 2

invasion at our border. As Governor of Texas and commander-in-chief of its military forces, I am using that Constitutional authority, as well as other authorization and Executive Orders to:

- Deploy the National Guard to safeguard our border and to repel and turn-back
immigrants trying to cross the border illegally,
- Deploy DPS to arrest and return to the border immigrants who crossed illegally and deploy DPS to arrest
illegal immigrants for criminal activity;
- Build a border wall in multiple counties on the border;
- Deploy gun boats to secure the border;

- Designate Mexican drug cartels as foreign terrorist organizations;
- Enter into a compact with other states to secure the border;
- Enter into agreements with foreign powers to enhance border security; and
- Provide resources for border counties to increase their efforts to respond to the border invasion.

I am also asking counties to join me in sending urgent messages to Congress reminding them that it is the federal government's responsibility to secure the border and to provide resources to do so. Congress should amend statutes like 18 U.S.C. § 242 to ensure that our Troopers and Guardsmen are not exposed to federal criminal prosecution for protecting Texas against illegal entry between the ports of entry.

You have an essential assignment: Use every available tool and strategy to fight back against the unprecedented invasion that Texas is seeing at our border. Until Congress acts or the Biden Administration does its constitutionally required job, Texas Guardsmen and Troopers must bear the burden of securing the border. You must continue to keep Texans and Americans safe and protect against an invasion of the southern border. I order you to use all resources and tools available to repel immigrants from attempting to cross illegally, arrest those who cross illegally and return them to the border, and arrest criminals who violate Texas law.

Sincerely,

Greg Abbott
Governor

------- End Reference 7 ------

The Evidence

Number 8

8. Reference:
Congress Request Refused

https://judiciary.house.gov/sites/evo-
subsites/republicans-
judiciary.house.gov/files/legacy_files/wp-
content/uploads/2022/11/2022-11-18-HJC-GOP-to-
Garland-DOJ.pdf

U.S. Congress House of Representatives
Committee on the Judiciary

First Letter
To:
The Honorable Merrick B. Garland
Attorney General
U.S. Department of Justice
November 18, 2022

Paragraph 2

Over the past twenty-one months, we have made
several requests for information and documents
concerning the operations and actions of the
Department of Justice. We reiterated and itemized

these requests in our recent letters of October 11, 2022, October 28, 2022, and November 2, 2022, which are enclosed for your convenience. To date, you have ignored these requests, or you have failed to respond sufficiently. Please be aware that if our requests remain outstanding at the beginning of the 118th Congress, the Committee may be forced to resort to compulsory process to obtain the material we require.

Second Letter
The Honorable Merrick B. Garland
Attorney General
U.S. Department of Justice
October 11, 2022

Paragraph 2
Since October 2021, we have sent over 100 letters to Departmental components
requesting documents and information regarding the Biden Administration's misuse of law enforcement resources.

1 To date, the Department has responded to these requests with only two half-page letters, and has not produced any of the requested documents or information. These letters do not sufficiently respond to our reasonable requests or alleviate our concerns.

Third Letter

The Honorable Merrick B. Garland
Attorney General
U.S. Department of Justice
October 28, 2022

Second Paragraph

Committee Republicans will continue to pursue these matters, including into the 118th
Congress if necessary. Accordingly, we reiterate our outstanding requests, which are itemized in the attached appendix and incorporated herein, and ask that you, as the custodian of all Departmental records, produce the entirety of the requested material as soon as possible but no later than November 11, 2022.

Forth Letter
The Honorable Merrick B. Garland
Attorney General
U.S. Department of Justice
November 2, 2022

We are conducting oversight of the Department of Justice's operations and actions concerning various matters. As a part of this oversight, Committee Republicans have sent letters to Departmental components requesting documents and information on several issues,1 including but not limited to the Department's targeting of journalists with Project

Veritas, the shuttering of the Department's China Initiative, the Department's one-sided enforcement of the FACE Act, and the Department's unprecedented raid on President Trump's residence. Our requests to you or your subordinates remain outstanding.

The American people deserve transparency and accountability from our most senior law enforcement official in the executive branch. Committee Republicans intend to continue to examine these matters, including into the 118th Congress if necessary. We reiterate our requests, which are itemized in the attached appendix and incorporated herein, and ask that you, as the custodian of all Department records, produce the entirety of the requested material as soon as possible but no later than November 16, 2022.

Furthermore, this letter serves as a formal request to preserve all existing and future records and materials in your possession relating to the topics addressed in this letter. You should construe this preservation notice as an instruction to take all reasonable steps to prevent the destruction or alteration, whether intentionally or negligently, of all documents, communications, and other information, including electronic information and metadata, that are or may be responsive to this congressional inquiry. This instruction includes all electronic messages sent using your official and personal accounts or devices, including records created using text messages, phone-based message applications, or encryption software

Jim Jordan
Ranking Member
cc:
The Honorable Jerrold L. Nadler
Chairman
Enclosure

The Honorable Merrick B. Garland
November 2, 2022
Page 3

Appendix: Outstanding Oversight Requests
June 8, 2021
1. Explain the Justice Department's current efforts to identify and prosecute individuals
involved in the assaults of Mr. Andy Ngo and other journalists in violation of federal
statutes securing their civil rights; and

2. Explain how the Justice Department, in coordination with other relevant federal and state
law enforcement agencies, is working to prevent individuals from engaging in violence
and intimidation designed to impair the free exercise and enjoyment of rights and
privileges that Mr. Andy Ngo and other journalists possess under the Constitution and
laws of the United States.

November 18, 2021

3. Explain when and how the FBI became aware of the diary purportedly belonging to
President Biden's daughter and describe when and why it opened an investigation into
the matter;

4. Provide copies of the search warrants, affidavits, and all other supporting documents
related to the FBI's search of residences of James O'Keefe and other current or former
journalists or employees of Project Veritas;

5. Explain the factual and legal predicate for the FBI to conduct raids at the homes of James
O'Keefe and other current or former journalists or employees of Project Veritas;

6. Describe the process the Department followed when obtaining subpoenas for the FBI to
obtain information from, or records of, James O'Keefe and other current or former
journalists or employees of Project Veritas, including whether you and/or any other
Department officials approved the decision to obtain such subpoenas;

7. Explain what steps, if any, the Department has taken or will take to investigate the

leaking of Project Veritas' information to the New York Times; and

8. Explain whether any official or employee of the Executive Office of the President
communicated with the Department and/or the FBI about investigating or searching the
residences of James O'Keefe and other current or former employees of Project Veritas.

February 17, 2022

1. All documents and communications referring or relating to the creation of the
Department of Justice's new domestic terrorism unit within the Counterterrorism Section
of the National Security Division;

The Honorable Merrick B. Garland
November 2, 2022

Page 4

2. All documents and communications between or among officials or employees of the
Executive Office of the President and the Department or National Security Division about
the creation of the new domestic terrorism office within the Counterterrorism Section of

71

the National Security Division;

3. An explanation as to why you decided to establish a new domestic terrorism office within
the Counterterrorism Section of the National Security Division, in contravention of prior
advice of career Department of Justice officials;

4. An explanation as to whether you or your staff consulted with the Department's career
lawyers in the Counterterrorism Section or elsewhere in the Department prior to the
establishment of this new office. If so, provide all recommendations and advice, both
formal and informal, that was made to the National Security Division about the newly
formed office;

5. An explanation whether the resources and personnel of this new domestic terrorism office
is being used or will be used to target concerned parents at local school board meetings;

6. Quantify the number of personnel assigned to the newly-formed domestic terrorism
office within the Counterterrorism Section of the National Security Division; and

7. Quantify the number of active domestic terrorism investigations, including by type of

case, for the period of January 1, 2021, to the present.

March 30, 2022:

1. All documents and communications referring or relating to the decision to end the
Department's China Initiative, to include an unredacted copy of the Department's three
month internal review initiated by you in November 2021;

2. An explanation as to whether you or your staff consulted with the Department's career
lawyers or other personnel in the Department prior to the decision to end the
Department's China Initiative. If so, provide all recommendations and advice, both
formal and informal, that was provided to you or your staff; and
3. An accounting of the Department's resources dedicated to combating national security threats posed by the People's Republic of China.

March 30, 2022:

1. All documents and communications referring or relating to the decision to end the
Department's China Initiative, to include an unredacted copy of the Department's three

73

month internal review initiated by you in November 2021;

2. An explanation as to whether you or your staff consulted with the Department's career
lawyers or other personnel in the Department prior to the decision to end the
Department's China Initiative. If so, provide all recommendations and advice, both
formal and informal, that was provided to you or your staff; and

3. An accounting of the Department's resources dedicated to combating national security
threats posed by the People's Republic of China.

April 27, 2022:

1. Preserve all records relating to the Department's disciplinary and personnel actions
against Deputy U.S. Marshals who defended federal property in Portland, Oregon from
far-left rioters in the summer of 2020.

June 23, 2022:

1. All documents and communications between or among the Department of Justice and the

Executive Office of the President referring or relating to the harassment and intimidation campaign outside justices' homes; and

2. All documents and communications between or among employees of the Department of Justice referring or relating to the harassment and intimidation campaign outside justices' homes, including those sent or received by employees of the United States Attorney's Office for the District of Maryland and the United States Attorney's Office for the Eastern District of Virginia.

August 15, 2022:

1. All documents and communications referring or relating to the execution of a search warrant on President Trump's residence;

2. All documents and communications referring or relating to the decision to seek a search warrant for President Trump's residence;

3. All documents and communications referring or relating to the use of confidential human source(s) in connection with the search of President Trump's residence;

4. All documents and communications between or among the Department of Justice, Federal Bureau of Investigation, or the Executive Office of the President about a search of President Trump's residence

5. All documents and communications between or among the Department of Justice, Federal Bureau of Investigation, or the United States Secret Service about a search of President Trump's residence;

6. All documents and communications between or among the Department of Justice, the Federal Bureau of Investigation, or the National Archives and Records Administration about a potential search of President Trump's residence

October 7, 2022:

1. All documents and communications between the U.S. Attorney's Office for the Eastern District of Pennsylvania and other components of the Department of Justice referring or relating to enforcement of the Freedom of Access to Clinic Entrances Act between May 2, 2022, and present;

2. All documents and communications between the U.S. Attorney's Office for the Eastern

District of Pennsylvania, the Department of Justice, or the Executive Office of the

President referring or relating to the Department's Reproductive Rights Task Force

3. All documents and communications between the U.S. Attorney's Office for the Eastern

District of Pennsylvania and the Department of Justice referring or relating to

investigations of attacks on pregnancy resource centers between May 2, 2022, and the

present;

4. All documents and communications referring or relating to the attack on the HOPE

Pregnancy Center in Philadelphia, Pennsylvania, that occurred on June 10, 2022; and

5. All documents and communications between the U.S. Attorney's Office for the Eastern District of Pennsylvania and the Federal Bureau of Investigation referring or relating to the arrest of Mark Houck

------- End Reference 8 ------

The Evidence

Number 9

9. Reference:
https://www.rga.org/wp-content/uploads/2021/09/Joint-Letter-to-President-Biden-to-meet-on-Border-09.20.21.pdf
September 20, 2021

President Joseph R. Biden, Jr.
The White House
1600 Pennsylvania Avenue NW
Washington, DC 20500

Dear Mr. President,

As chief executives of our states, we request a meeting with you at The White House to bring an end to the national security crisis created by eight months of unenforced borders. The months-long surge in illegal crossings has instigated an international humanitarian crisis, spurred a spike in international criminal activity, and opened the floodgates to human traffickers and drug smugglers endangering public health and safety in our states. A crisis that began at our southern border now extends beyond to every state and requires immediate action before the situation worsens.

The negative impacts of an unenforced border policy on the American people can no longer be ignored. Border apprehensions are up almost 500% compared to last year, totaling more than 1.3 million—more people than the populations of nine U.S. states. Approximately 9,700 illegal apprehensions have prior criminal convictions. Cartels and traffickers are making $14 million a day moving people illegally across the border. More fentanyl has been seized this fiscal year than the last three years combined— almost 10,500 pounds of fentanyl when only 2 milligrams prove fatal. This is enough to kill seven times the U.S. population.

Despite the lack of federal action to reverse the crisis, many states have stepped up and committed unprecedented resources to support the security of our national border. We have heard directly from our constituents about the damage this crisis has caused in our states, and it is our duty as elected officials to act swiftly to protect our communities, as it is yours.

While governors are doing what we can, our Constitution requires that the President must faithfully execute the immigration laws passed by Congress. Not only has the federal government created a crisis, it has left our states to deal with challenges that only the federal government has a duty to solve. Our immigration system may be complicated and complex, but the solution to ending the border crisis is simple and straightforward. As President, you have the ability to take action to protect America, restore security, and end the crisis now.

September 20, 2021

Therefore, we come directly to you seeking an open and constructive dialogue regarding border enforcement on behalf of U.S. citizens in our states and all those hoping to become U.S. citizens. We must end the current crisis and return to border operations that respect the laws of our land and the lives of all people, including those in our states looking to the federal government to enforce and protect our nation's borders.

Due to the emergent crisis, we respectfully request a meeting as soon as your schedule allows within 15 days. While we know your responsibilities as Commander in Chief are substantial, ending the national crisis and securing our states must be a priority.

Sincerely,

Governor Doug Ducey State of Arizona
Governor Mike Dunleavy State of Alaska
Governor Greg Abbott State of Texas
Governor Kay Ivey State of Alabama

Governor Asa Hutchinson State of Arkansas
Governor Ron DeSantis State of Florida
Governor Brian Kemp State of Georgia
Governor Kim Reynolds State of Iowa
Governor Tate Reeves State of Mississippi
Governor Pete Ricketts State of Nebraska
Governor Brad Little State of Idaho
Governor Larry Hogan State of Maryland
Governor Mike Parson State of Missouri
Governor Chris Sununu State of New Hampshire
Governor Eric Holcomb State of Indiana
Governor Charlie Baker State of Massachusetts
Governor Greg Gianforte State of Montana
Governor Doug Burgum State of North Dakota
Governor Mike DeWine State of Ohio
Governor Kevin Stitt State of Oklahoma
Governor Henry McMaster State of South Carolina
Governor Kristi Noem State of South Dakota
Governor Bill Lee State of Tennessee
Governor Spencer Cox State of Utah
Governor Jim Justice State of West Virginia
Governor Mark Gordon State of Wyoming

------- End Reference 9 ------

The Evidence

Number 10

Reference: 10
https://www.federalregister.gov/documents/2025/01/29/2025-01948/declaring-a-national-emergency-at-the-southern-border-of-the-united-states

Proclamation 10886 of January 20, 2025

Declaring a National Emergency at the Southern Border of the United States

A Proclamation

By the authority vested in me as President by the Constitution and the laws of the United States of America, I hereby proclaim:

America's sovereignty is under attack. Our southern border is overrun by cartels, criminal gangs, known terrorists, human traffickers, smugglers, unvetted military-age males from foreign adversaries, and illicit narcotics that harm Americans, including America.

This invasion has caused widespread chaos and suffering in our country over the last 4 years. It has led to the horrific and inexcusable murders of many innocent American citizens, including women and children, at the hands of illegal aliens. Foreign criminal gangs and cartels have begun seizing control of parts of cities, attacking our most vulnerable citizens, and terrorizing Americans beyond the control of local law enforcement. Cartels control vast territories just south of our southern border, effectively controlling who can and cannot travel to the United States from Mexico. Hundreds of thousands of Americans have tragically died from drug overdoses because of the illicit narcotics that have flowed across the southern border.

This assault on the American people and the integrity of America's sovereign borders represents a grave threat to our Nation.

Because of the gravity and emergency of this present danger and imminent threat, it is necessary for the Armed Forces to take all appropriate action to assist the Department of Homeland Security in obtaining full operational control of the southern border.

To protect the security and safety of United States citizens, to protect each of the States against invasion, and to uphold my duty to take care that the laws be faithfully executed, it is my responsibility as President to ensure that the illegal entry of aliens into the United States via the southern border be immediately and entirely stopped.

As Commander in Chief, I have no more solemn duty than to protect the American people.

NOW, THEREFORE, I, DONALD J. TRUMP, President of the United States of America, by the authority vested in me by the Constitution and the laws of the United States of America, including sections 201 and 301 of the National Emergencies Act (50 U.S.C 1601 et seq.), hereby declare that a national emergency exists at the southern border of the United States, and that section 12302 of title 10, United States Code, is invoked and made available, according to its terms, to the Secretaries of the military departments concerned, subject to the direction of the Secretary of Defense. To provide additional authority to the Department of Defense to support the Federal Government's response to the emergency at the southern border, I hereby declare that this emergency requires use of the Armed Forces and, in accordance with section 301 of the National Emergencies Act (50 U.S.C. 1631), that the construction authority provided in section 2808 of title 10, United States Code, is invoked and made available, according to its terms, to the Secretary of Defense and, at the discretion of the Secretary of Defense, to the Secretaries of the military departments. I hereby direct as follow.

Section 1 Deployment of Personnel and Resources.

The Secretary of Defense, or the Secretary of each relevant military department, as appropriate and consistent with applicable law, shall order as many units or members of the Armed Forces, including the Ready Reserve and the National Guard, as the Secretary of Defense determines to be appropriate to support the activities of the Secretary of Homeland

Security in obtaining complete operational control of the southern border of the United States. The Secretary of Defense shall further take all appropriate action to facilitate the operational needs of the Secretary of Homeland Security along the southern border, including through the provision of appropriate detention space, transportation (including aircraft), and other logistics services in support of civilian-controlled law enforcement operations.

Sec. 2 Additional Physical Barriers.

The Secretaries of Defense and Homeland Security shall immediately take all appropriate action, consistent with law, including 10 U.S.C. 2214, to construct additional physical barriers along the southern border. To the extent possible, the Secretaries of Defense and Homeland Security shall coordinate with any Governor of a State that is willing to assist with the deployment of any physical infrastructure to improve operational security at the southern border.

Sec. 3 Unmanned Aerial Systems.

The Secretary of Transportation and the Federal Communications Commission shall, consistent with applicable law, consider waiving all applicable Federal Aviation Administration and Federal Communications Commission regulations or policies, respectively, that restrict the Department of Homeland Security's ability to counter unmanned aerial systems within 5 miles of the southern border.

Sec. 4 Revision of Policies and Strategies

The Secretary of Defense and the Secretary of Homeland Security, in consultation with the Attorney General, shall take all appropriate action, consistent with law, to prioritize the impedance and denial of the unauthorized physical entry of aliens across the southern border of the United States, and to ensure that use of force policies prioritize the safety and security of Department of Homeland Security personnel and of members of the Armed Forces.

Sec. 5 Revocation. Proclamation 10142 of January 20, 2021 (Termination of Emergency With Respect to the Southern Border of the United States and Redirection of Funds Diverted to Border Wall Construction), is hereby revoked.

Sec. 6 Reporting Requirement. (a) With in 30 days of the date of this proclamation, the Secretary of Defense shall submit to the President, through the Homeland Security Advisor, a report outlining all actions taken to fulfill the requirements and objectives of this proclamation; and

(b) Within 90 days of the date of this proclamation, the Secretary of Defense and the Secretary of Homeland Security shall submit a joint report to the President about the conditions at the southern border of the United States and any recommendations regarding additional actions that may be necessary to obtain complete operational control of the southern border, including whether to invoke the Insurrection Act of 1807.

Sec. 7 General Provisions.

(a) Nothing in this proclamation shall be construed to impair or otherwise affect:

(i)the authority granted by law to an executive department or agency, or the head thereof; or

(ii)the functions of the Director of the Office of Management and Budget relating to budgetary, administrative, or legislative proposals.

(b)This proclamation shall be implemented consistent with applicable law and subject to the availability of appropriations.

(c) This proclamation is not intended to, and does not, create any right or benefit, substantive or procedural, enforceable at law or in equity by any party against the United States, its departments, agencies, or entities, its officers, employees, or agents, or any other person.

IN WITNESS WHEREOF, I have hereunto set my hand this twentieth day of January, in the year of our Lord two thousand twenty-five, and of the

Independence of the United States of America the two hundred and forty-ninth.

Donald Trump

Filed 1-28-25; 8:45 am]

[FR Doc. 2025-01948

Billing code 3395-F4-P

------- End Reference 10 ------

Conclusion and Internet Petition

After considering the January 25, 2017 Executive Order 13768 of President Trump, it was a major effort with eighteen sections of executive actions to get control of the southern border as required by law. In contrast, the January 20, 2021 Executive Order 13993 by President Joseph R. Biden revoked President Trump Executive Order 13768.

The obvious intent of President Trump was to get the southern border under control, while in contrast, the obvious intent of President Biden was to get the southern border out of control with only three sections which created violations in the U.S. Constitution and federal law.

The actions of President Biden open borders provided great Aid and Comfort to the aliens entering the southern borders through his open border policy enacted by his Executive Order 13993. By revoking the regulated border by Trump to an unregulated open border, this dramatically increased the volume of entries to the point of overwhelming the capabilities of the border patrol to control the southern borders according and required by federal law and the United States Constitution. This policy remained in effect until President Trump reelection.

It is very significant to consider that President Biden office length was four years.

With each year consuming 365 days and President Biden was in office totaling four years created the obvious 1,460 opportunities to create policy to get the southern border under control as demanded by federal law and the United States Constitution. President Biden decided not to control the southern border everyday consistently for 1,460 days. The obvious question is WHY? He could have forgot or perhaps his values told him to keep the southern borders open and out of control. Could that be consistent with the policy and purpose of the National Democratic Party and the Biden Executive Office leaders? Did they do anything to stop this out-of-control policy that could destroy the United States, or is that what they wanted done?

You must agree that there is only one way to find an answer to these questions.

That is, you must copy, print, sign and mail the petition.

Remember, and never forget. Born in this country, you are a citizen of the United States of America and thereby part owner of this country. Did President Biden open border policy and his Executive office along with the Democratic Party all providing great Aid and Comfort to the aliens entering the southern borders TO YOUR COUNTRY and therefor my question is: DOES THAT MAKE YOU ANGRY?

As citizen of the United States of America and thereby part owner of this country, I am asking you to preserve, protect and defend the United States Constitution against both foreign and domestic enemies of the United States of America and:

Either write the petition on your paper in your hand writing OR
copy and paste using your computer onto a word document or a simple text file and print on your printer.

So, please use your current date. Sign the document and include your city and state.

Mail To:

U.S. Department of Justice

950 Pennsylvania Avenue, NW

Washington, DC 20530-0001

Petition

Current Date: _____

To: To United States Department of Justice
    Attorney General
    950 Pennsylvania Avenue, NW
    Washington, DC 20530-0001

Subject: Request Treason Grand Jury Criminal Investigation

Purpose:

Whether President Biden, his administration, and others in the Democratic party committed treason against us, we the people of the United States of America from January 2021 through January 2025, and therefore we ask for a federal grand jury to investigate reasonable cause for a criminal indictment and issue, if necessary, against those responsible.

Failure to act will leave the opportunity for treason to return and next time we may lose the country. We asked for your help to save The United States of America.

Your signature

_____

Your City and State

_____

* * * *   Petition End   * * * *

Remember what Benjamin Franklin said,
"We have a republic if we can keep it."

The founding fathers created the republic now it is
our job to keep it.
Therefore, your participation is required to save the
United States of America.
I ask for your participation with this Internet
Petition.

Most Sincerely yours,
Michael Carlson
Huntsville Alabama

http://holyspiritfacetoface.com/